Glacier

on my mind

" *Far away in northwestern Montana, hidden from view by clustering mountain-peaks, lies an unmapped corner— the Crown of the Continent.* "

George Bird Grinnell,
George Bird Grinnell: A Biographical Sketch

Photography by Michael Sample

FALCON™

A veil of clouds lifts from the face of Going-to-the-Sun Mountain

" *My first feeling is for the mountains that rise steep from the plains. From the roads that skirt their high bases one looks down into chasms and sees the floating white of clouds. The effect is of heights and depths and space that set the spirit soaring. The spirit wings free, too, at the sight of azure lakes or the bear grass that blows nearly everywhere. The sense of adventure and awe is heightened when the visitor sees eagles, or bighorn sheep, or wild goats, or, possibly, a grizzly and her cub. . . . The word for these rewards to sight and soul is glory, or majesty, or grandeur. Over the centuries nature, in travail, has delivered them. They make human concerns unimportant.* "*

A.B. Guthrie, Jr., introduction to
Glacier-Waterton Explorers Guide

The splendor of fall in vivid radiance at Lower St. Mary Lake on the Blackfeet Indian Reservation

The chilly waters of McDonald Creek rush down from the Continental Divide into McDonald Lake

Mount Gould towers above Josephine Lake

A whitetail doe among lush summertime vegetation

A glacier lily unfolds its modest elegance

Sunrise burnishes the morning fog on the east side of Glacier National Park

" The sun had not risen. Along the horizon was a supernatural light—a glow of pale yellow, mingled with touches of red and gold. It spread upwards towards the zenith; the glow grew stronger and the sun rose. "

Walter McClintock,
The Tragedy of the Blackfoot

Blanketflowers and the "big sky" at Many Glacier

Hiking the Iceberg Lake Trail

The seldom-seen Jones' columbine
among trailside rocks

❝ You may walk the same trail a dozen times and not tire of the view. I have given up wondering why. I know only that these are mountains a man might grow old with, and that mountain-fever never diminishes but only changes its look, as a forest does over many years. ❞

Greg Beaumont,
Many-storied Mountains:
The Life of Glacier National Park

Falls tumble into the placid waters of Lake Frances

Looking down onto the heights of the Continental Divide from the south ridge of Mount Custer, with Mount Cleveland rising to the left

On the Garden Wall below Grinnell Overlook, this mountain goat looks very much at home

Twin mountain goat kids

Majestic Reynolds Mountain rises to 9,125 feet, towering above the foggy forest

Exposed rock layers in Waterton Lakes National Park

The first sun of the day inflames the face of Grinnell Point

Glacial movement helped carve the noble Swiftcurrent Mountain

Hikers read the visitors' log and chat with the keeper at the Swiftcurrent Mountain fire lookout

Full of life and on top of the world

“ *Listen, Old Man! . . .Give to all Mountaineer people full life. Make their bodies strong to enjoy the Great Outdoors which their spirits crave. Old Man, give them strong legs and sure feet. Help them to hear the Great Spirit speaking in the mountain tops.*

"We welcome you Mountaineers. O-ky! Ever welcome in Glacier National Park of the great land of the Red Men. ”

Chief Eagle Calf

Skipping rocks at St. Mary Lake

A great horned owlet scrutinizes the forest from its perch

A frog and a dragonfly visit a yellow water lily

Autumn light shimmers on the waters of Upper St. Mary Lake

An aspen leaf glows like a gold doubloon

A carpet of many hues in a Glacier forest

A piebald forest of tamarack and pines announces autumn in Glacier

Sometimes the sun comes to earth along Going-to-the-Sun Road

The porcupine and its 30,000 quills

" It is doubtful if any other road in America can in the same distance unfold . . . such a grand array of beautiful forests, dashing torrents, wonderful gorges and valleys, towering cirques, and a vista of bold-needled mountians and serrated escarpments. "

Stephen T. Mather,
first director of the National Park Service

A moment of awe marks the birth of a new day at Lake Sherburne

Alpenglow paints the top of the world along the Continental Divide

A single wisp of cloud heralds day's end for this ice-chilled pond

A fall storm wraps snow around a snag above Hidden Lake

The best protection: ptarmigan in its winter camouflage

The angled peak of Bearhat Mountain after an early winter storm

The waters of Lake McDonald grow still in early winter as the snows descend;
Mount Vaught and McPartland Mountain rise in the background

Fall colors grace a hillside beneath Mount Wilbur

A frost settles on a dogwood bush

A frond of huckleberry

" The rocks were of all shades, from pale gray, through green and pink, to dark red, purple and black, and against them stood out the pale foliage of the willows, the bright gold of the aspens and cottonwoods, the vivid red of the mountain maples and ash, and the black of the pines. . . . Over all arched a leaden sky, whose shadows might dull, but could never efface, the bewildering beauty of this mass of color. "

George Bird Grinnell, 1885
*Grinnell's Glacier: George Bird Grinnell
and Glacier National Park*

A swallowtail butterfly visits an orange hawkweed

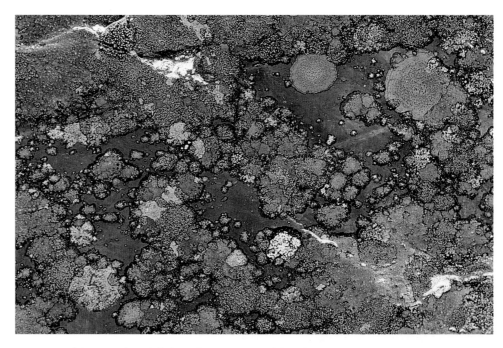

Many-colored lichen form a surreal landscape on a single rock

Snow bridges span a small creek on the Garden Wall in summer

Light dances in the clear waters of Apikuni Creek

" Eventually, all things merge into one, and a river runs through it. The river was cut by the world's great flood and runs over rocks from the basement of time. On some of the rocks are timeless raindrops. Under the rocks are the words, and some of the words are theirs.

"I am haunted by waters. "

Norman F. Maclean,
A River Runs through It

Rushing current polishes the rocks in the Middle Fork of the Flathead River

Under the surface of gurgling Baring Creek

The luxuriance of spring comes to Two Medicine Country in southern Glacier National Park

41

"*Aquamarine blue, topaz yellow, and garnet red: The wildflowers of Montana's Glacier National Park are as brilliant as a dowager's jewel box.*"

Rebecca Sawyer-Fay,
"Montana's Crown Jewels,"
Country Living

Shooting star flowers

Many shades of green grace a meadow at Round Prairie

Lady's luncheon

An idyllic creek bottom scene beneath Mount Rockwell

Lush gardens welcome summertime guests to Glacier Park Lodge

Penstemon catches the light

A handful of Indian paintbrush and a sky full of mountains near Logan Pass

Rocky Mountain iris

Butterfly in a camas

Horsemint

Pink fairy slipper

A black bear frolics among lupine and blanketflower in spring

We finally passed from the forest into an open basin surrounded by lofty peaks. I marvelled at the luxuriant growth of the grass and the variety and brilliant colouring of the flowers, caused by the abundant precipitation. There was the beautiful dark blue flower of the camass, the violet red of the wild geranium, the violet blue of the western virgin's bower, and the yellow of the wild parsley; also forget-me-nots, mountain lilies, spring daisies, and blue larkspurs.

Walter McClintock,
The Old North Trail, or
Life, Legends and Religion of the Blackfeet Indians

St. Mary Lake on a calm day

Wilbur Creek nourishes a vivid spread of mosses

Bearhat Mountain angles sharply above Hidden Lake in the heart of Glacier National Park

Two marmots keep lookout
in the afternoon sun

A silver-tipped grizzly bear lumbers through a field in search of food *Michael H. Francis photo*

Bear claw marks in bark

This beargrass meadow near Mount Oberlin and Mount Cannon is prime grizzly habitat

The long shadows of summer evenings come to Hidden Lake

Bird Woman Falls cascades across overhanging rocks

Smooth paddling on Kintla Lake

Coming ashore after a dance across the water

Give a month at least to this precious reserve. The time will not be taken from the sum of your life. Instead of shortening, it will indefinitely lengthen it and make you truly immortal. Nevermore will time seem short or long, and cares will never again fall heavily on you, but gently and kindly as gifts from heaven.

John Muir,
Our National Parks

Two friends have fun on Lake McDonald

The lights of Many Glacier Hotel shimmer on the surface of Swiftcurrent Lake

Visitors catch the jaunty jammer buses at Lake McDonald Lodge   *Inga Spence/Tom Stack & Associates*

Rafters find a thrill on the Middle Fork of the Flathead River *Montana Raft Company photo*

A community of beargrass surrounds Oldman Lake beneath Flinsch Peak

Dark shadows of Mount Cleveland rise above the glacier-fed Angels Pool

Kintla Creek swirls around a bend through some of the most pristine country in the world

A bull elk forages alone below Mount Cannon

“ Softly carried on the wind over a high mountain basin, the shrill whistle of a bugling bull carries more depth of feeling, more subtle grace and more awe-inspiring power than any manmade music could ever hope to make. ”

Mark Henckel,
"Bugle Boy: Autumn's Grand Notes,"
Montana Magazine

The bull elk, one of the most majestic residents of Glacier Park
Donald M. Jones photo

Elk sometimes feed on bark in the toughest days of winter

Evening settles in over Swiftcurrent Lake

Wild Goose Island resembles a castle in the distant light on St. Mary Lake

Morning sun brightens the edge of a clearing

Billion year old rock ripples, at the base of Clements, give mute testimony to the Park's oceanic beginnings

A welcome rest spot along McDonald Creek

The sea, even the prairie, has a certain fascination; but the lure of the mountains is something more potent than anything else in nature. In sunshine or in storm, glorified by the purple haze of summer, or the scintillating snows of winter, they quicken the deepest springs of your being. No other temple of worship has the power to bring one more truly into harmony with the sublime.

Margaret Thompson,
High Trails of Glacier National Park

Glacial scraping sculpted this lake bed below Sperry Glacier

View through a shower of meltwater from an ice cave near Sperry Glacier

Striated layers tell the geologic history of the Sperry Glacier terrain

A wintry Gunsight Mountain looms above dormant Sperry Chalet and frozen Lake Ellen Wilson

" *Here are cañons deeper and narrower than those of the Yellowstone, mountains higher than those of the Yosemite. Some are rounded and some square-topped, some are slender pinnacles, and others knife-edged and with jagged crests, each one a true sierra. . . . Along their verdureless slopes slow-moving ice rivers still plow their deliberate way, relics of mightier glaciers, the stiffened streams of which in a past age fashioned the majestic scenery of to-day.* "

George Bird Grinnell
"The Crown of the Continent,"
The Century Magazine

Cracks in a frozen lake paint a surreal picture

&& *What justifies the national parks? First of all, silence. In any park three minutes' walk will permit you to be alone in the primeval, and this single fact is enough to justify the entire national-park system. Moreover you will enjoy the intimacy of nature as your forefathers knew it. . . .*

"The national parks preserve not only the organic relationship of nature, they also preserve the extremes of natural spectacle and natural beauty. **&&**

Bernard De Voto,
"Footloose In Democracy" in
*Mirror of America: Literary
Encounters with the National Parks*

Feathered flower of frost on ice

Ethereal light over Going-to-the-Sun Mountain

It was a day of great moving clouds. Clouds with personalities came striking out of chasm bed-chambers, clouds overtook us and enveloped us. . . . Presently there was not a particle of view above us except cloud, and no view below except of the rocks at our feet and the cloud-filled ravines.

Stephen Graham,
Tramping with a Poet in the Rockies

Tufted clouds on Heavens Peak glow under the full moon

Iceberg Lake earns its name year-round

A cloud obscures the peak of Going-to-the-Sun Mountain in early morning

A sea of summits rewards climbers atop Mount Wilbur in Swiftcurrent Valley *Brian Kennedy photo*

A bicyclist's view of the Weeping Wall along
Going-to-the-Sun Road *Scott Spiker photo*

66 *I remember as a child reading or hearing the words 'The Great Divide' and being stunned by the glorious sound, a proper sound for the granite backbone of a continent.* 99

John Steinbeck,
Travels with Charley

A bighorn ram seems to enjoy the sun on the Garden Wall

Bighorn sheep graze an alpine meadow with the distinct shape of Bishops Cap in the distance

The delicacy of the pasque flower

" When [Old Man] made the bighorn with its big head and horns, he made it out on the prairie. It did not seem to travel easily on the prairie; it was awkward and could not go fast. So he took it by one of its horns, and led it up into the mountains, and turned it loose; and it skipped about among the rocks, and went up fearful places with ease. So he said, 'This is the place that suits you; this is what you are fitted for, the rocks and the mountains.' "

George Bird Grinnell,
Blackfoot Lodge Tales:
The Story of a Prairie People

Water from snowmelt feeds this creek on Gunsight Mountain all year round

The blue waters of Lake of the Seven Winds and Pitamakan Lake, beneath McClintock Peak,
look like gems dropped among the rocks

A ptarmigan changes from summer to winter colors
from the bottom up

*66 The supreme glory of Glacier National
Park is in its wealth of water. Fed by glaciers
and melting snows from a thousand drifts
along the continental divide, its swift-flowing
streams and sparkling cascades are everywhere,
usually leading to or from a vivid tarn or
mountain lake. . . . It is impossible adequately to
describe the romantic charm, the exquisite
beauty and the extraordinary variety of these
magnificent lakes. 99*

Warren L. Hanna,
Montana's Many-Splendored Glacierland

81

A bouquet of colorful canoes awaits summertime paddlers at Cameron Lake in Waterton Lakes National Park

66 *Why are all the
beautiful lakes high up—
the most exquisite the
highest up? Is it the
cussedness of nature that
all the most beautiful
things are most hidden
and hardest to attain?* 99

Agnes C. Laut,
Enchanted Trails of Glacier Park

The townsite of Waterton perches on the shore of beautiful Waterton Lake

The Prince of Wales Hotel, in Waterton Lakes National Park, blends in with the spires behind it

Backpackers board a boat at the Crypt Lake Trail landing in Waterton Lakes National Park

A moment to remember on Crandell Lake in Waterton Lakes National Park

The angled lines of history are evident to hikers along the Crypt Lake Trail

Bison forage freely in the Buffalo Paddock just outside of Waterton Lakes National Park

The earth displays its many colors to hikers in Waterton's Red Rock Canyon

Wildflowers grace the hanging valley of Preston Park while the sharp summit of Reynolds Mountain rises in the distance

A bighorn ram calmly ignores respectful hikers

Even the smallest ski run is irresistible

It would be easy to stay indefinitely in Glacier; it's one of those places that cannot be exhausted, where every stride changes the light and the view and adds to your store of wilderness experience.

Michael Robbins,
High Country Trail: Along the Continental Divide

Siyeh Pass Trail wends through an elegant carpet of glacier lilies beneath Matahpi Peak

A camper-friendly deer shares its backyard with backpackers

An angler finds the ultimate retreat at Angels Pool, tinted aquamarine by glacial melt

A boardwalk protects the fragile tundra from damaging footprints at Logan Pass

A grizzly bear appears to be sightseeing in a spring meadow *Michael H. Francis photo*

Two proud flags fly at the Logan Pass Visitor Center

Reynolds Mountain towers over the rushing waters of Reynolds Creek

Quaking aspens in the height of their finery on the way to Iceberg Lake

Spent fireweed signal the first approach of summer's end at McDonald Creek

A young bull moose frolics in Kootenai Lakes while foraging on water plants

Yellow water lily blossoms bob in Winona Lake

An elegant lace of lichen decorates the intertwined twigs of lodgepole pine

This gnarled cottonwood stands in mute witness to the ferocity of fire

Sofa Mountain appears to stretch out comfortably over the rolling hills of Waterton Lakes National Park

The Steller's jay

An alder stand along Bowman Creek

This cabin was once the summer retreat of painter Charles M. Russell

66 *It would do my soul a world of good to spend a few days off in those timber clad hills around Lake McDonald with someone who appreciates nature.* 99

Charlie Russell, 1920

Each work of nature is a work of art

The setting sun showers a stand of birches in gold at Belton Hills

Ripe huckleberries ready for picking

Moss adorns the folds of a western red cedar trunk

Dogwood and Rocky Mountain maple give these northern forests much of their vivid color in the fall

Blanketflowers and lupine spread like a festive skirt before Apikuni Mountain

Fireweed is one of the first flowers to bloom after a forest fire

❝ Here, serrated ridges and horn-shaped peaks reign over a jumble of turquoise lakes, waterfalls, cascades, river valleys, hanging gardens, and alpine meadows. Born of geologic and glacial violence, this random landscape couldn't be more perfect had it been designed and executed by Michelangelo. Like the ocean, its sheer scope has a way of putting humanity in its place. ❞

Norma Tirrell,
Montana

A long, spectacular ridge points the way to Mount Cleveland in the Lewis Range

A majestic meeting of mountain and light along Swiftcurrent Creek, with Grinnell Point in the background

Of all things created, these mountains only have escaped the domination . . . of man. . . . The valleys are scarred by the plow, ridged by the trail maker, and guttered by the taker of water; but the mountains are still as God made them, and to be near them is to be on the pathway to peace.

Chief Plenty Coups

Beargrass, a distinctive and common flower in Glacier and Waterton Lakes

A nanny and kid peer curiously from their safe perch

“ *Goats. . . . One by one, they launched themselves off the cliff and hung suspended for a long moment above a thousand feet of dense, blue space. They might have been white birds in the circle of my binoculars, buoyed up by the momentum of their leap. . . . The way they moved was something to believe in; falling was not a concept they knew or feared.* ”

Beth Ferris, from "The Gatekeepers" in
*Montana Spaces: Essays and
Photographs in Celebration of Montana*

Bald eagle in flight across a blue Montana sky   *Robin Brandt photo*

acknowledgments

The publisher gratefully acknowledges the following sources:

Page 1 quoted in *George Bird Grinnell: A Biographical Sketch,* by Cynthia Parsons. © 1992 by University Press of America, Inc., Lanham, Maryland.

Page 3 from the introduction to *Glacier-Waterton Explorers Guide,* by Carl Schreier. © 1984 by Carl Schreier; Homestead Publishing, Moose, Wyoming.

Page 7 quoted in *Stars Over Montana: Men Who Made Glacier National Park History,* by Warren L. Hanna. © 1988 by Glacier Natural History Association, West Glacier, Montana.

Page 9 from *The Tragedy of the Blackfoot,* by Walter McClintock. Southwest Museum Papers No. 3, Southwest Museum, Los Angeles, April 1930.

Page 11 from *Many-storied Mountains: The Life of Glacier National Park,* by Greg Beaumont. Division of Publications, National Park Service, U.S. Department of the Interior, 1978.

Page 15 from "On the Edge of Earth and Sky," by Douglas H. Chadwick. Published in *National Geographic,* April 1995.

Page 19 quoted in *The Mountaineer,* Volume Seven, 1914.

Page 25 quoted in *The Majestic Land: Peaks, Parks & Prevaricators of the Rockies & Highlands of the Northwest,* by Eric Thane. © 1950 by the Bobbs-Merrill Co., Inc., Indianapolis, Indiana.

Page 30 from *Winter of the Sleeping Giants,* by William F. and Lynda Shiffman. © 1992 by Shiffman and Shiffman Enterprises, Missoula, Montana.

Page 35 quoted in *Grinnell's Glacier: George Bird Grinnell and Glacier National Park,* by Gerald A. Diettert. © 1992 by Gerald A. Diettert; Mountain Press Publishing Company, Missoula, Montana.

Page 38 from *A River Runs through It,* by Norman Maclean. © 1976 by the University of Chicago Press, Chicago.

Page 41 from "Montana's Crown Jewels," by Rebecca Sawyer-Fay. Published in *Country Living,* August 1994.

Page 47 from *The Old North Trail, or Life, Legends and Religion of the Blackfeet Indians,* by Walter McClintock. © 1992 by the University of Nebraska Press, Lincoln, Nebraska.

Page 51 from *The National Parks Portfolio,* by Robert Sterling Yard. Government Printing Office, Washington, D.C.

Page 52 from *Through Glacier Park in 1915,* by Mary Roberts Rinehart. © 1983 by Roberts Rinehart Publishers, Boulder, Colorado.

Page 57 from *Our National Parks,* by John Muir. © 1901 by John Muir; Houghton, Mifflin Co., Boston.

Page 62 from "Bugle Boy: Autumn's Grand Notes," by Mark Henckel. Published in *Montana Magazine,* September/October 1995.

Page 67 from *High Trails of Glacier National Park,* by Margaret Thompson. © 1936 by The Caxton Printers, Ltd., Caldwell, Idaho.

Page 71 from "The Crown of the Continent," by George Bird Grinnell. Published in *The Century Magazine,* September 1901.

Page 73 from *Mirror of America: Literary Encounters with the National Parks.* © 1989 by the National Park Foundation; Roberts Rinehart Publishers, Boulder, Colorado.

Page 74 from *Tramping with a Poet in the Rockies,* by Stephen Graham. © 1922 by D. Appleton and Company, New York.

Page 77 from *Travels with Charley,* by John Steinbeck. © 1962 by John Steinbeck; The Viking Press, New York.

Page 79 from *Blackfoot Lodge Tales: The Story of a Prairie People,* by George Bird Grinnell. Published 1962 by University of Nebraska Press, Lincoln, Nebraska.

Page 81 from *Montana's Many-Splendored Glacierland,* by Warren L. Hanna. © 1976 by Superior Publishing Co., Seattle.

Page 83 from *Enchanted Trails of Glacier Park,* by Agnes C. Laut. © 1926 by Robert M. McBride & Co., New York.

Page 89 from *High Country Trail: Along the Continental Divide,* by Michael Robbins. © 1981 National Geographic Society, Washington, D.C.

Page 99 quoted in *Theodore Roosevelt the Naturalist,* by Paul Russell Cutright. © 1956 by Harper & Brothers, New York.

Page 101 quoted in *Charles M. Russell, Word Painter,* edited by Brian Dippie. © 1993 Amon Carter Museum, Fort Worth, Texas.

Page 105 from *Montana,* by Norma Tirrell. © 1991 by Compass American Guides, Inc., Oakland, California.

Page 107 quoted in *The Majestic Land: Peaks, Parks & Prevaricators of the Rockies & Highlands of the Northwest,* by Eric Thane. © 1950 by the Bobbs-Merrill Co., Inc., Indianapolis, Indiana.

Page 109 from *Montana Spaces: Essays and Photographs in Celebration of Montana,* edited by William Kittredge. © 1988 by The Montana Land Alliance; Nick Lyons Books, New York.

Page 112 from *Through Glacier Park in 1915,* by Mary Roberts Rinehart. © 1983 by Roberts Rinehart Publishers, Boulder, Colorado.

The sun bids an august farewell to Chief Mountain

“ *Cities call—I have heard them. But there is no voice in all the world so insistent to me as the wordless call of the Rockies. . . . Those who go once always hope to go back. The lure of the great free spaces is in their blood.* ”

Mary Roberts Rinehart,
Through Glacier Park in 1915